# THE AMAZON RAINFOREST
## AND ITS PEOPLE

**Marion Morrison**

**Wayland**

# PEOPLE
## · AND PLACES ·

*The Amazon Rainforest and its People*

*The Arctic and its People*

*The Prairies and their People*

*The Sahara and its People*

First published in 1993 by Wayland (Publishers) Ltd
61 Western Road, Hove, East Sussex, BN3 1JD, England

© Copyright 1993 Wayland (Publishers) Ltd

**British Library Cataloguing in Publication Data**
Morrison, Marion
The Amazon Rainforest
I. Title  II. Series
981.06

ISBN 0 7502 0484 2

Typeset by Dorchester Typesetting Group Ltd
Printed and bound in Italy by G. Canale & C.S.p.A.

**Book editors:** Liz Wyse and Paul Bennett
**Series editor:** Cally Chambers
**Designer:** Mark Whitchurch

**Consultant:** Roger Hammond, Chief Executive of
The Living Earth Foundation.

**Acknowledgements**
The publishers would like to thank the following for
allowing their photographs to be reproduced in this book:
Sylvie Cordaiy 9 top (J. A. Miles); Sue Cunningham 14
bottom; Eye Ubiquitous 9 bottom (N. Howarth), 10 (Julia
Waterlow); Gaia Foundation 44; Mary Evans Picture Library 5
bottom, 17; Nasa/Science Photo Library 41; Edward Parker
contents page, 12, 13, 22; South American Pictures 6 both, 8
both, 21, 25, 26 left, 31 top, 32, 37 (Edward Parker), 18 top;
Still Pictures 5 top, 18 inset, 19, 24, 27, 45 (Edward Parker);
Still Pictures/Mark Edwards 14 right, 15 both, 16, 23, 26
right, 28, 29 both, 31 bottom, 32, 34, 35, 36, 39, 42; Tony
Stone Worldwide title page (Ary Diesendruck); Wayland
Picture Library cover.
Artwork by Peter Bull (4, 11, 20, 30, 33 bottom, 36) and
Tony Smith (7, 33 top, 38, 40, 43).

**Cover:** A group of *caboclos* have cleared a small area of
rainforest beside the Maderia river. They grow bananas which
are taken by passing boats to the nearest town for sale.

**Title page:** The Iguassu Falls hotel complex, Brazil. The
spectacular scenery of Amazonia is beginning to attract
tourists. However, there are worries about the environmental
impact of a tourist 'invasion'.

**Contents page:** A rubber tapper's house in a rainforest
clearing. The house is built from palm trees and thatched
with palm fronds. Food – manioc, maize, rice, sugar-cane –
is grown in forest gardens nearby.

# C O N T E N T S

# ·THE·AMAZON·
# ·BASIN·

Amazonia is the name given to the vast region in South America that is drained by the Amazon river and its tributaries. Covering about 7 million square kilometres, the Amazon basin is similar in size to the USA. Seventy per cent of Amazonia is in Brazil, but the source of the Amazon river is a tiny stream high in the Andes mountains in Peru. The remaining part of the river basin lies in countries that border Brazil, namely French Guiana, Surinam, Guyana, Venezuela, Colombia, Ecuador, Peru and Bolivia.

The Equator runs right through Amazonia giving it a tropical climate. Although the temperatures are high, much of Amazonia is extremely humid because of very high rainfall. In fact, it rains so much over the region that over a thousand tributaries drain the basin and flow into the Amazon River. Some of the them are over 1,600 km long, and one, the Madeira, is over 3,200 km in length. In terms of the area drained and the amount of water carried away, the Amazon and its tributaries make up the largest river system in the

*The Amazon is the largest river system in the world. It drains a basin of more than 7 million sq km and has more than 1,000 tributaries.*

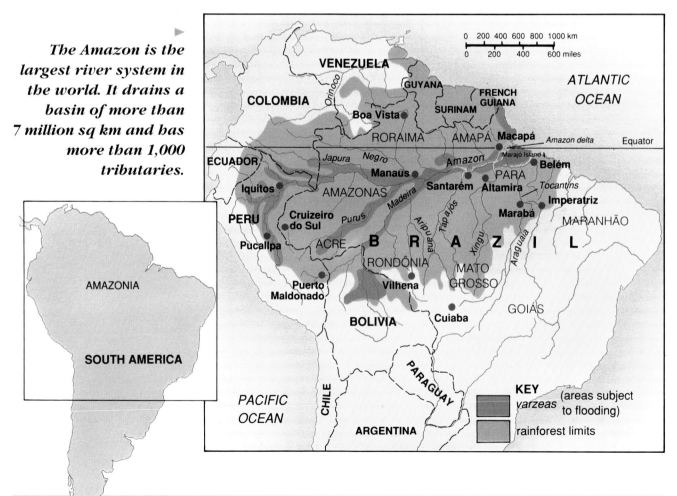

4

world. It finds its way 6,400 km across South America to the Atlantic coast, where the river mouth is over 241 km wide.

It is estimated that the Amazon and its tributaries carry about one-sixth of the world's fresh water draining from rivers, and that an astonishing 770 billion litres of water flow into the Atlantic Ocean every hour. It pours into the Atlantic with such force that fresh water is still mixing with the salt water of the ocean up to 160 km off the coast.

*The forest canopy covers thousands of square kilometres of Amazonia.*

*Von Humboldt visited South America in the nineteenth century, and was fascinated by the luxuriant vegetation and abundance of species in the rainforest.*

## EARLY EXPEDITIONS

In 1542, the Spanish soldier, Francisco de Orellana, and his companions were the first Europeans to come down the Amazon when they completed a journey of almost 3,220 km from the Napo, a tributary in Ecuador. They survived many hazards along the way, and it is believed that de Orellana named the river after coming across fierce female warriors, whom he compared to the Amazons – a race of women warriors from Greek mythology.

For almost two hundred years from the time of de Orellana, the region was closed to outsiders by the Spanish and Portuguese. Then, in 1736, a Frenchman, Charles Marie de la Condamine, led a scientific expedition, to be followed sixty years later by a German scientist, Alexander von Humboldt. During his long journey, von Humboldt collected information about the geography of the area and the many animals and plants he found there. During the nineteenth century, several people interested in nature visited the region. One naturalist, Richard Spruce from England, spent seventeen years there, studying and collecting thousands of plants.

▲
*A mangrove tree on Marajo Island at the mouth of the Amazon river.*

## HABITATS

Even today, scientists working in the vast area of the Amazon river basin face an enormous challenge. The region contains not only the world's largest and probably oldest rainforest, but also a variety of other habitats depending on the local climate and geography. These include the swampy mangroves to the east, the open savannah to the north, the *cerrado* forest of small twisted trees broken by grasslands to the south, and the cloud forests of the Andes to the west. Another feature of Amazonia are the *varzeas*, or flood plains, created when tributaries flood during the annual rainy season, leaving fertile deposits

▲
*The grassland of the north-eastern Amazon.*

of alluvium, or silt, on the river banks. *Varzeas* provide rich soils which have been farmed for centuries and on which some of the finest rainforests grow. Of all the varied habitats within the Amazon region, it is the rainforests that cover the largest area and for which Amazonia is most well known.

# ·THE·RAINFOREST·

Seen from an aircraft, the rainforest stretches endlessly to the horizon and is so dense that the ground cannot be seen. The light falling on the rainforest canopy encourages the crowns, or tops, of the trees to grow thick and leafy, and other species of plants to grow in the treetops. Mosses, orchids, climbing plants, vines and bromeliads all add to the abundance of life that steals the light from the levels of forest beneath. The canopy almost forms a separate world in which certain birds, monkeys and insects can live in isolation from the rest of the rainforest.

At the mid-forest level there are other trees whose leafy crowns barely reach the height at which the giant trees begin to branch. In the gloom of the forest floor below, tall shrubs fill the spaces between the bare tree trunks that seem to spread out endlessly on every side. Rope-like climbing plants called lianas struggle upwards to the canopy, sometimes thicker than the supporting trees. Some of the trees are supported by odd-shaped trunks and long roots that weave a pattern just beneath the soil's surface, while other trees stand on dozens of stilt-like roots.

## A Fragile Balance

**Emergent trees grow taller to capture direct sunlight.**

**Rainforest canopy: monkeys and birds live high up in the rainforest.**

**Mid-forest level: smaller trees fill the spaces between giant tree-trunks.**

**Lianas; rope-like plants struggle upwards to reach the sunlight.**

**Low-forest level; the vegetation is dense and there is hardly any sunlight.**
**Buttress roots support tall trees. Dead leaves and wood cover the forest floor. Insects and fungi break it down to a fertile compost, which feeds the soil.**

monkey

toucan

puma

capybara

The massive root systems of the rainforest trees take up the nutrients from the compost formed on the forest floor. The soil also provides a rich start for seedlings which may find enough space and sunlight to grow and compete with the towering giants above them. The soil continually recycles the nutrients and energy of the forest. The roots of the dense vegetation and the overhead canopy protect the soil and its nutrients from being washed away by heavy rain.

*Many of the trees of the rainforest have tall smooth trunks that rise for over 30 m without branching.*

*The leaves and branches of the forest floor decompose quickly under the combined action of fungi, bacteria and insects.*

Trees include the giant Brazil-nut, the tall silk-cotton – which has seed capsules containing a soft, cottony floss called kapok – hardwoods such as mahogany, and a rich assortment of palms with strong fibres and oil-producing nuts.

Because the rainforest is near to the Equator, where sunlight and warmth are constant all the year round, the climate remains hot and there are no seasons. As a result, the forest is rich and green at any time of the year, and trees and plants can be found at various stages in their life cycles. Many trees bear smooth waxy leaves which allow rainfall to run off quickly, helping to prevent damaging fungi growing on the trees. The canopy protects the forest from heavy rainfall.

As the trees shed their leaves continually and dead wood falls to the forest floor, a thin bed of damp debris builds up. This, together with the tropical climate, makes ideal living conditions for insects, tiny fungi and bacteria which quickly break down the plant material into a rich compost or mulch. Some of the fungi are like miniature toadstools, while others resemble mould on old bread and are so small that they can only be seen under a microscope. Despite their size, these agents of decay can break down both animal and plant debris within a matter of days or weeks. Even enormous tree trunks will disappear in a year or two.

## THE VARIETY OF LIFE

The rich vegetation is part of a food web that includes a whole variety of animal life; jaguars and pumas of the cat family, species of New World monkeys, wild pigs, deer, alligators, snakes, rodents and insects. Some of the more unusual species include armadillos, anteaters, sloths, the tapir and the capybara which, being about the size of a small pig, is the world's largest rodent. In the canopy a wide variety of birds make their home, including toucans, macaws, parrots and humming-birds.

*Capybara, the world's largest rodents, are at home in water or on land.*

*This rainforest spider is brightly coloured as a warning to predators.*

*The caiman, a South American relative of the crocodile, was very common in much of Amazonia until the early 1960s, when demand in Europe and the USA for its skin almost caused its extinction.*

Many of the diverse species of the Amazon rainforest still remain unidentified by scientists. Studies indicate that a patch of rainforest just 6 km square contains as many as 2,500 species of flowering plant, 750 species of tree, 400 species of bird, 150 species of butterfly, 100 species of reptile and 60 species of amphibian. The number of species of insects can only be guessed at, but probably runs into tens of thousands. Not surprisingly, the Amazon region is acknowledged as one of the richest and most valuable ecosystems on earth, but despite this, it has been stripped of the resources it provides with hardly a thought to conservation for the future.

The great biodiversity, or variety of animal and plant life, has taken many millions of years to evolve. One theory suggested that this extraordinary diversity developed be-cause the Equatorial climate remained stable for such a long time. However, more recent evidence shows that in the past two million years, areas of rainforest in Amazonia have actually shrunk when ice ages spread at the poles, disrupting the world's climate. At times, relatively small areas of rainforest were surrounded by expanses of grassland and small bushes. Within these separate areas, animals and plants continued to evolve in different ways. Then, as the climate changed again, these areas of rainforest joined up, bringing together the different species that had been evolving in isolation. Estimates vary widely, but Amazonia probably contains at least 10 per cent of all animal species in the world, and about 2,000 species of trees, which is about ten times the number found in northern forests.

# · PEOPLE · OF · THE · RAINFOREST ·

The Amazon rainforest is home to various tribes of forest Indians. Between three and five million Indians were thought to be living in the Amazon forests at the time European settlers arrived in the sixteenth century. By the beginning of the twentieth century, less than a million survived. Many Indians died as result of being taken into slavery, but the main reason for the dramatic fall in numbers was that the Indians had no immunity against unfamiliar European diseases such as small-pox and influenza. Today, the number of Indians has fallen further, and it is thought that there are less than 200,000 of them living in small, scattered communities throughout the rainforest. Even these people's survival is threatened by the steady destruction of their homes and lifestyles.

To many forest-dwelling Indians, the rain-forest is a sacred place, home to the spirits that guide them through their daily lives. It provides everything that they need, including food, shelter, medicine and clothing. Over the centuries, they have developed a way of living that exists in harmony with their rain-forest environment.

*At least 500 different forest peoples live in the Amazonian rainforest. This map shows the location of the main Indian lands included in this book.*

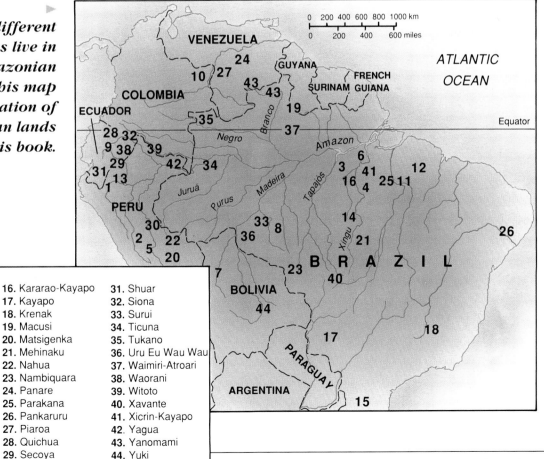

**Indian tribes**

| | | |
|---|---|---|
| 1. Aguaruna | 16. Kararao-Kayapo | 31. Shuar |
| 2. Amuesha | 17. Kayapo | 32. Siona |
| 3. Arara | 18. Krenak | 33. Surui |
| 4. Arawete | 19. Macusi | 34. Ticuna |
| 5. Ashaninka | 20. Matsigenka | 35. Tukano |
| 6. Asurini | 21. Mehinaku | 36. Uru Eu Wau Wau |
| 7. Chimane | 22. Nahua | 37. Waimiri-Atroari |
| 8. Cinta Larga | 23. Nambiquara | 38. Waorani |
| 9. Cofan | 24. Panare | 39. Witoto |
| 10. Cuiva | 25. Parakana | 40. Xavante |
| 11. Gavioes | 26. Pankaruru | 41. Xicrin-Kayapo |
| 12. Guaja | 27. Piaroa | 42. Yagua |
| 13. Huambisa | 28. Quichua | 43. Yanomami |
| 14. Juruna | 29. Secoya | 44. Yuki |
| 15. Kaingang | 30. Shipibo | |

*The fleshy, swollen roots of manioc are one of the staple crops of Amazonia.*

### FARMING THE FOREST

Throughout Amazonia, the Indians have come to use methods of cultivation that do not damage the forest. They know that the soils of the rainforest are thin and fragile and so will only support crops for a few years. They use a method of shifting cultivation in the forest which is known as 'slash and burn' – clearing a small patch of rainforest for temporary farming before moving on again. If too large an area were to be cut down and burnt, the soil would lie open to heavy rainfall. Nutrients would be leached, or washed, out of the soil and the soil itself would be at risk of being eroded, or swept away.

The Kayapó tribe of central Brazil limit this damage by planting varieties of sweet potato that are resistant to fire. By planting them before the burning takes place, the potatoes are able to take up nutrients that would otherwise be washed away. The Kayapó also allow weeds to grow, in order to hold on to nutrients and protect the otherwise bare soil. They know which areas of the new plot are most suited to different plants, so vegetation quickly grows and protects the soil. The tribe spread natural fertilizers on to the cleared land. They use ash from burnt trees and the nests of termites and biting ants, which are high in nutrients. In order to control leafcutter ants that would destroy their crops, the Kayapó plant a variety of banana tree as

hedging. This is the home of a particular kind of wasp that drives the ants away.

The principal crop grown throughout Amazonia is manioc, which is used to make cassava bread – the staple diet of many tribes. In its natural state, manioc is poisonous, but by a process of soaking in water, grating and squeezing, it can be made edible. Other crops include maize, yams and plants that provide fibres or medicines.

*Flat manioc cakes are made by sifting grated manioc on to a large, heated metal pan. The cakes are then shaped and toasted until crisp.*

▼

## THE RAINFOREST PROVIDES

After a tribe has moved on to another part of the forest, the clearing is soon seeded by the surrounding trees and plants, and the area becomes overgrown. However, members of the tribe continue to return to the clearing to harvest the fruit, fibres and medicines of the trees and plants that are growing there. Often they will plant species of trees whose fruit will attract animals, not only because the animals provide food, but also because they introduce, through their droppings, the seeds of fruit or forest trees that can be harvested.

As well as collecting plants, fruits, berries, nuts, honey and spices from the rainforest, the Indians hunt for fish and animals such as tapirs, wild pigs, rodents, monkeys and birds. They make blowguns and bows for hunting from a black and extremely tough palm wood. The tips of their arrows are dipped in curare, a deadly poison that they extract from a vine. Cooking is simple and the meat is often grilled over hot embers. Sometimes it is mixed with the fleshy underground stems or roots of plants and cooked in turtle or armadillo shells, or in the dried, outer skin of large fleshy fruits called gourds.

The rivers, which many tribes respect as much as the rainforest itself, are rich with fish

*A Campa Indian hunts with a bow made from palm-wood. His arrow is from a straight cane and is tipped with a wooden head for stunning birds.*

*Kayapó women collect Brazil nuts deep in the rainforest.*

*These Campa Indians use aluminium and plastic utensils brought by traders.*

*A Kayapó child whose skin has been painted using natural dyes.*

of many kinds. Among the Tukano Indians of Brazil, it is forbidden to prepare the river banks for the cultivation of crops, as they believe that the river banks belong to the fish. Undisturbed sections of the rivers, regarded as the resting place of their ancestors, provide excellent places for fish to breed.

In areas where clay is found, the traditional Indians make pottery containers in which to keep seeds, vegetable dyes and other items gathered from the forest. The houses of the Indians are made from wood and thatch, with strong lianas or tree bark used for tying rafters. Pieces of palm are cut for use as nails to secure timbers. Very often the huts are built on stilts to raise them above the forest floor.

For clothing, some tribes use layers of fibre taken from under the bark of certain trees, but most Indians weave the soft, fluffy fibres of wild or cultivated cotton on hand-made looms. For decoration the Indians select natural dyes from the forest, such as the red dye from the annatto plant and the blue dye from the genipa plant, and paint their bodies and clothes with them. Necklaces and bracelets are made from seeds, and head-dresses from bird feathers.

*The people of Amazonia have faith in natural products. Some are used for healing, others for spiritual purposes.*

### THE HEALING FOREST

Over the centuries, the Indians have discovered that many of the rainforest plants make good medicines. Some can be used as painkillers, or to heal wounds and cure fevers, or for helping to reduce or increase people's ability to have children. Quinine, a substance that is found in the bark of the cinchona tree, is used to treat the deadly disease malaria. Western scientists have discovered how to make quinine artificially and now it is manufactured on a large scale in factories. Another of the rainforest's resources, curare, which tribes use to poison their arrowheads for hunting, can be used to relax the muscles of patients in surgical operations. Now that the importance of the rainforest as a source of new medicines is recognized in the industrialized countries, scientists have become concerned that the destruction of the rainforest will mean that many medicinal plants will become extinct. If the traditional lifestyles of the Indians disappear, their valuable knowledge of the rainforest will die too.

### RIGHTS TO THE LAND

The first Indians are thought to have arrived in the Amazon from the north some 10,000 to 20,000 years ago. In all this time, they have never thought of the land as their property – there was no need to do so because they saw themselves as part of the forest. But now, with the invasion of settlers and people looking to extract valuable resources from the land and transforming the rainforest, the Indians have been forced to change their attitudes and fight for their right to this land.

As well as the Indians, there are other groups of people that have lived in the rainforest for generations. Their traditional ways of life are also under threat. These people include the *seringueiros* or rubber tappers, and *caboclos*, people such as Brazil-nut gatherers, woodcutters and fishermen.

# · THE · RUBBER · BOOM ·

Among the taller trees in the rainforest is the species of rubber tree known as *Hevea brasiliensis.* Long before the arrival of the European explorers, the Indians were using the white sticky fluid, or latex, from beneath the bark of the trees to make balls and water carriers. In 1736 Charles de la Condamine was the first person to introduce the elastic material to Europe, recognizing its value as a waterproof covering. By the 1800s, thousands of rubber bottles and boots made in Amazonian workshops were being exported, and factories in Europe were making rubber goods from imported latex.

*Small-scale exploitation of Amazonian rubber dates back to the early 1800s. However, the material was difficult to use – in cold weather the raw rubber became brittle and stiff, in hot weather it became soft and sticky. In the 1840s a new process, called vulcanization, was patented. Sulphur was mixed with rubber, producing a hard-wearing material which kept its 'bounce' when hot or cold.*

*Just beneath the bark of the rubber tree is a softer tissue that is rich with a creamy liquid called latex.*

*When the bark is cut the liquid flows out and is gathered by rubber tappers.*

In the beginning of the twentieth century, rubber was in demand for bicycle tyres and other industrial uses, and this resulted in the Amazon rubber boom. Tens of thousands of people went to the Amazon hoping to make their fortune from tapping rubber trees. Small towns and ports, such as Manaus, 1,600 km up the Amazon, and Belém, at the mouth of the river, grew rich and prosperous.

## A HARD LIFE

For people working in the new rubber industry, the work was almost like slavery. The tappers had to borrow money from the landowners to buy the provisions and tools they needed to work on the rubber trails. Few were able to earn enough to repay the money, and so each year they sank further and further into debt. They were forced to spend long hours searching the rainforests for rubber trees. Then, in their simple palm-leaf shacks, the tappers smoked layers of liquid latex on a paddle over a fire before the large balls of brown rubber could be sent down the river. There, the traders made huge profits from the sale of rubber to Europe and the USA.

The landowners employed people to oversee the collection of rubber and these people pressurized the Indians to work as tappers. When they refused to work or tried to escape they were often killed. Faced with this threat to their way of life, many tribes disappeared deeper into the forest.

**END OF THE BOOM**

Demand for rubber continued to grow and the tappers were forced to go deeper into the rainforest to find more rubber trees. The price of the rubber rose quickly. Although different species of rubber tree grew in other parts of the world, *Hevea brasiliensis* was thought to produce the best latex. In the 1880s, an Englishman, Henry Wickham, sent about 70,000 seeds out of Brazil to the Royal Botanical Gardens at Kew in England. Only 7,000 seedlings grew, and were sent to Sri Lanka where they were planted in swampy conditions and most died. But a handful survived and were the basis of the great rubber plantations of Malaya. Free from the tropical pests of the Amazon, the trees grew well. The transfer was so successful that by 1913, the supply of rubber from the new plantations was greater than that of the Amazon rainforests and the rubber boom in South America came to an end.

Attempts were made to create Brazilian rubber-tree plantations that would compete with the rubber produced in Southeast Asia. One such project was called Fordlandia, because it was paid for by the American motor-car maker, Henry Ford. However, because the rubber trees were planted too close together, the Amazonian plantations became affected by a fungus that spread easily and weakened the trees, leaving them open to attack by other fungi and also insect pests. As a result, the Amazonian plantations failed and allowed those in Southeast Asia to become even more successful. Today, rubber tappers in Amazonia continue to work as they did before the nineteenth-century boom – on trees growing wild in the rainforest.

*Most Amazonian rubber is still produced in the way it was a hundred years ago. The latex collected in the forest is slowly dripped on a pole which is turned by hand in the smoke of a palm-nut fire. The latex hardens to a tough rubbery mass.*

# · R O A D S · I N T O · T H E · F O R E S T ·

The Amazonian region represents over half of Brazil's territory, yet twenty-five years ago less than 3 million of the 70 million population lived there. In all of Brazil's neighbouring countries too, only a fraction of the total population lived in the region covered by the Amazon. As a result, government after government in these countries has looked for ways to move people into the rainforest regions. Central to such plans has been the construction of new roads and the improve-

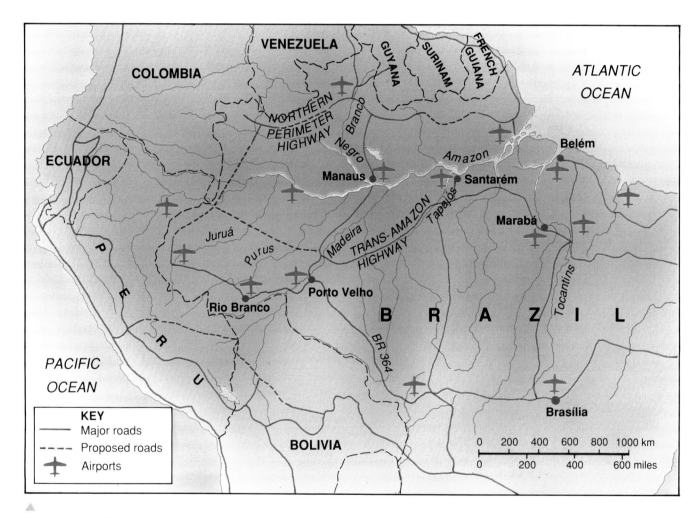

**Major road-building schemes are intended to open up remote areas of the rainforest for settlement and development.**

*Since the late 1950s major road projects, such as this route to north Brazil, have been completed throughout Amazonia.*

ment of transport in the region, and much money has been invested in road building.

In the past sixty years, each new Brazilian government has sought ways of developing the Amazon and the rainforest. In the 1930s, for example, President Getúlio Vargas tried to make the rubber industry prosperous again with a programme called 'March to the West'. But few people were attracted to move into the area and so the scheme failed.

From the 1940s onwards, various organizations were set up to develop the Brazilian rainforests. The first of the highways was completed in 1960. Running from Belém to the then-new capital called Brasília, the highway was supposed to open up the Amazon to development projects and settlers. Areas of the rainforest were cleared along the route of the highway, but by the mid-1960s it was obvious that the response was disappointing and the region remained largely untamed.

From 1964, the military government in Brazil decided that the time had come for the organized development of the Brazilian Amazon. It seemed to provide an answer to the growing number of poor people who were flooding into cities such as São Paulo and Rio de Janeiro. Hardships caused by drought in the north-east and the spread of large-scale farming in the south drew them to the cities. Most of the people were unable to find work there, and they survived in poor housing that sprang up on the outskirts of the cities.

## THE TRANS-AMAZON HIGHWAY
With much publicity, the plan to construct the 5,450-kilometre Trans-Amazon Highway was announced in 1971. It would run due west from north-east Brazil to the town of Porto Velho in Rondônia, about 508 km south of, and largely parallel with, the Amazon river. The World Bank and the InterAmerican Development Bank gave financial support. Settlers were offered huge incentives to

*Road-building projects have made remote areas of West Brazil accessible for settlers.*

develop the region, such as loans, financial aid for equipment and relief from taxes.

Families were offered 97-hectare pieces of land in the cleared forest, as well as housing and a small salary for a few months. There were plans for schools, health clinics and other services too. But the tens of thousands of settlers that were expected failed to come forward, and of those that did, many gave up after only a few months because life in the Amazon was too hard. The scheme has been such a failure that it has been estimated that the Trans-Amazon Highway, together with other, smaller highways built at the same time, have cost the Brazilian government and its backers $39,000 per person settled.

**DISASTER FOR THE ENVIRONMENT**
Another highway has led to ecological disaster, simply because of its success at reaching into the rainforest. This highway, known as BR364, runs from the south of Brazil and through the frontier states of Rondônia and Acre. About a million settlers were attracted to Rondônia between 1970 and 1980, largely as a result of a lot of publicity and misleading claims of fertile land. Huge areas of the rainforest in the region were cut down and burned. The devastation is believed to be the worst anywhere in Amazonia. Not only has a large area of rainforest habitat been lost, but the soil has quickly become eroded and been turned into poor agricultural land.

When the first highways were being built in the 1950s, colonists were encouraged to move into the Brazilian Amazon as small farmers and ranchers. Few people expected the speed and extent of the destruction of the rainforest that followed.

Due to a lack of proper scientific research, the settlers believed that if they cleared the land of trees, the soil would be able to produce good crops for many years without the use of fertilizers. Unlike the Indians, who had developed their farming methods over thousands of years, they did not realize that the soil would become exhausted after only a few years. They found that, in order to make a living, they had no option but to move on and cut down more trees. The Indians' slash and burn techniques of farming leave small patches of rainforest which recover after a few years, but the colonists' farming methods were crude and laid large areas of rainforest to waste. Without the cover of vegetation, the precious soils were washed away by heavy rainfall and flooding, and crops could not grow. Once this has happened it is very difficult for the land to recover.

*This valley in Peru has been cleared, but few farmers know how to conserve the soil.*

**This Amazon forest has been cleared for cattle. Brazil-nut trees are protected by law.**

There were other problems facing the colonists. Not only were they at risk from many infectious diseases, but the rainforest also harbours pests that destroyed their crops. Instead of farming a variety of crops just to provide food for their families – which is known as subsistence farming – many of the settlers were persuaded to concentrate on producing a single crop, such as rice, in return for cash. But costly fertilizers were needed to keep up the output of cash crops and colonists had to accept the low prices that the government had fixed for their crops. They found that settling in the rainforest did not bring the prosperity they had hoped for.

## NEW RIGHTS TO THE LAND

Although some colonists gained written ownership of the land on which they settled, a great many could not. Instead, they relied on an ancient Brazilian law that gives right of possession to anyone who stays unchallenged on a plot of land for a year and a day, whilst trying to make the land productive. Unfortunately, clearing the forest was seen by the colonists as the simplest way of showing that they intended to farm the land and large areas were cut down unnecessarily.

Worried by how much land was being 'grabbed', the Brazilian government introduced a law known as the 'law of the 50'.

This forbade landowners to cut down more than 50 per cent of the trees on their property. However, people soon got round this law, especially the large landowners who either sold off the uncut piece of land, or gave it to another member of the family to clear 50 per cent and pass on the remainder.

As the value of land rose because of the wealth to be gained from minerals and timber within the region, land grabbing became more common. It was often accompanied by violence, and some wealthy landowners even forced their smaller neighbours to resettle elsewhere.

## RAISING CATTLE

Some of the worst examples of land grabbing took place during the effort to develop ranching. In the 1950s, the Brazilian government encouraged people to raise cattle, and in the 1960s this policy was continued by the military government. Meat is a central part of the Brazilian diet. It was hoped that locally produced beef would keep the price of meat down and so help the poorer people.

However, like the small farmers, the ranchers that moved into the area did not understand that, once cleared of trees, the Amazon soil would not remain fertile for long, and the nutrients would wash away with the heavy rains. It has been estimated that in some parts of the forest, up to 25 hectares of land is needed to support one head of cattle. Smoke-filled skies became commonplace as the land was cleared and the felled trees burnt. Large areas of the Amazon were cleared before ranchers realized that it was uneconomic to raise cattle on the land. Today they continue to buy up the rainforest, sometimes still for ranching, but mostly because the land is now more valuable for its minerals and timber.

*Cattle and a plantation of banana-like plantains have replaced the rainforest in this part of Pará State in eastern Amazonia.*

▲

*Ilzamar, the young widow of the murdered Chico Mendes.*

◄

*Manaus, is a busy port almost 1,600 km from the Atlantic.*

## DISSATISFACTION

Not surprisingly, the settlement of the rainforest has led to conflict between the traditional people of the forest and the newcomers. For centuries, Indian peoples have been pushed around by outsiders trying to make money from the land. Organizations set up by governments in recent years to protect the Indians have failed to make much difference and many tribes have had to look after their own interests. The Indians have tried attacking the colonists and their livestock, but they have suffered many casualties because the settlers can afford to defend themselves with guns.

Recently, some Indians have joined forces with the rubber tappers, whose livelihood has also been threatened by the clearance of the rainforest. Together, particularly in Rondônia and Acre, they have had some success in holding on to their land, but not without some of them being hurt. Their fight has caught the world's attention in recent years, as many of the tappers speak Portuguese and have been able to talk about their concerns to the press and to world leaders. Chico Mendes, the rubber tapper's leader, was murdered in 1988 partly because of the publicity he had raised about rainforest destruction. His work, backed by television and press reports, persuaded governments and organizations to support the rights of the Indians

*A* **caboclo** *cleans freshly-caught catfish beside an Amazon tributary in Brazil.*

and rubber tappers, and to control the destruction of the rainforest.

Unhappy at the harsh lifestyle in the cleared rainforests, many thousands of the people living in Amazonia are moving to the towns. Porto Velho in Brazil and Pucallpa in Peru are examples of towns that have found it difficult to cope with the large numbers of people that have arrived. There is no easy solution to the problem and people often end up living in poor conditions and find it hard to get work.

Despite all the money that has been poured into the development of ranching and farming, Brazil still imports meat and cannot provide enough food for its people. Fresh fish is becoming an increasingly important part of people's diet in Amazonia. Scientists estimate that there are as many as 3,000 species of fish in the rivers of the region, and some are very large. A catfish, for example, can weigh as much as 136 kg. However, the fish are now also threatened by the destruction of the rainforest and according to local fishermen some good food fish are becoming scarce. During the rainy season, the rainforest floor in some areas gets flooded, and this allows the fish to feed on the fruit and forest litter. Where the rainforest has been cleared, the fish do not get the food they need to survive. Again, the well-being of the people relies on what happens in the rainforest.

# · T H E · T I M B E R ·
# · I N D U S T R Y ·

One of the other causes of deforestation in Amazonia is the timber industry. Fine hardwood trees, such as mahogany, are cut down for export to richer industrialized countries of the world. Mahogany is often used for window frames, doors and even lavatory seats. Britain is the principal importer of Brazilian mahogany, closely followed by the USA. Other timbers are removed for use in the construction industry and for the making of plywood.

In the rainforest, some species of tree usually grow tens of metres apart. In order to cut just one valuable tree and drag it to the river or road for transportation, dozens of other trees of little or no economic value are cleared to make a route for powerful tractors. Many hectares of forest are destroyed for the sake of a few trees. Sometimes the loggers use small aircraft to pinpoint an area rich with good quality mahogany and then carve a path through the forest to get to it. Whilst this selective logging saves trees and encourages the recovery of the forest, it is expensive and only worthwhile in areas where the mahogany is plentiful, such as in the south of Pará State in eastern Brazil, and in Rondônia on the Bolivian border.

Loggers also purchase timber from ranchers and settlers who are cutting down the rainforest to use the land for cattle or crops. As the land is cleared, valuable trees are

*A Peruvian settler clears land for farming. Almost everywhere in Amazonia chain saws made in Brazil or Japan have replaced the axe.*

*When trees are removed, soil soon becomes infertile.*

*Planks of mahogany are stacked for export at Belém.*

removed while all the uneconomic wood is burnt. The rancher is happy because the money received for the timber pays for the cost of clearing the trees. In a similar way, when the forest is cleared for mining or dam projects, the timber can make extra money for the developers.

Plywood factories are often built beside a river, so that large tree trunks of up to 1.5 m across can be floated downstream from the rainforest, and hauled straight to the ply-wood-making machinery. The trunks are cleaned and then turned against a sharp blade that skims the wood away in thin sheets. At the end of the process, the core of the trunk, cut down to just under 0.5 m across, is thrown on to a waste heap or used to make charcoal. The thin sheets of wood are glued together under heat and pressure to make strong plywood.

Timber is one of the most valuable resources in the Amazon rainforest. Unlike some materials, such as fossil fuels, which have taken many millions of years to form, trees can usually grow to maturity in a few decades. They are often regarded as a renew-able resource because once cut, other new trees will grow. However, most of the timber industry in the Amazon is not managed in this way. When land has been cleared, it is left as barren wasteland. Nevertheless, some attempts are being made to protect the fragile soil so that new trees will grow and some reseeding projects in Brazil have shown that it is possible to encourage the rainforest to recover. Unfortunately, there are still relative-ly few incentives to encourage such projects, although there is an increasing awareness among some timber companies that reforesta-tion is essential for their future.

# · M I N E R A L · WEALTH · AND · ENERGY ·

*I*t has been known for a long time that Amazonia contains valuable mineral deposits but it wasn't until more recent decades that their extraction became big business.

## THE GRANDE CARAJÁS PROJECT

In the 1960s, the largest-known deposit of high-grade iron ore in the world was found in the mountains of the Serra dos Carajás in Brazil. Nearby, geologists discovered deposits of copper, gold, bauxite, nickel and other minerals.

By the 1980s, the Grande Carajás project, involving about 550 million hectares of the Brazilian Amazon, had become a huge development scheme and the centre of a pro

gramme called PoloAmazonia. PoloAmazonia involved the creation of fifteen poles, or zones, designed to attract people and industry to particular areas of the Amazon region. New airports and a network of roads were built to make transport easy in the region, and an 860-kilometre railway was laid down to carry the iron ore from the Serra dos Carajás mine to a new port at São Luis on the Atlantic coast for export by sea. Hydroelectric dams were built to generate electricity and new towns and cities were planned to house the workers. The government also provided money for fertilizers and scientific advice in order to encourage a successful local agricultural industry.

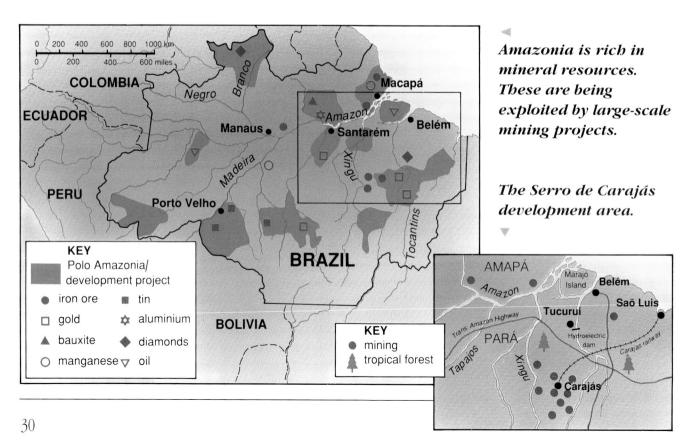

*Amazonia is rich in mineral resources. These are being exploited by large-scale mining projects.*

*The Serro de Carajás development area.*

*The natural resources of Amazonia are now being exploited in places that were once too remote. This iron ore mine in Carajás is 890 km from the Atlantic coast.*

The cost of the project ran into billions of dollars and was funded by the Brazilian government, the USA, Japan, some European countries and the World Bank. In an effort to avoid protests from environmental agencies, the planners established a protected area of rainforest around the iron-ore mine. However, although only one huge pit has been dug to extract the ore today, over a dozen places have been marked in the Carajás project area for future sites. The pits will be so large that it will be impossible to fill them in. Large areas of habitat will be lost and the landscape scarred for many years.

There have also been an increasing number of small scale iron-ore smelters built in the area. These rely on charcoal to heat the ore, and charcoal is made from wood. There are plans to establish plantations of eucalyptus trees to provide the wood but, in the meantime, huge areas of the rainforest are being cut down at a rate of between 1,036 and 1,554 square kilometres a year for the production of charcoal. Even if eucalyptus plantations do come to provide the wood necessary for charcoal making, the variety of

*Scraps of mahogany from a sawmill are turned into charcoal by local children.*

species of the natural rainforest will be lost as well as the habitat for many living creatures.

Further devastation has been caused in the Carajás project area by ranchers clearing the land, and there are plans for cement plants and factories that will process metals, causing even more damage to the rainforest. The Indians in the area have suffered as a result. Although some reserves have been established, several thousand Indians have already been pushed off their lands.

**FINDING ENERGY**

In order to supply power to the Carajás project area, the Tucuruí hydroelectric dam was built nearby on a large Amazon tributary called the River Tocantins. Bad planning led to the filling of the reservoir behind the dam before any of the trees had been removed. As the wood has rotted under the water, a greenhouse gas called methane has been released. This has created a worrying environmental problem, not only because of the size of the flooded area (the reservoir covers 3,885 square km) but also because methane is known to be many times worse than carbon dioxide as a greenhouse gas.

Hydroelectric power is often considered to be a good, 'clean' method of generating electricity, mainly because it does not cause pollution. But hydroelectric projects can be harmful to the environment in other ways. The plan proposed by Brazil's state electricity company to build over eighty plants in the Amazon region has been widely criticized,

*The largest hydroelectric dam in Amazonia is on the Tocantins river in Brazil.*

*The sometimes disastrous environmental consequences of building hydroelectric dams are often overlooked.*

**Mosquitoes breed on the still waters of the reservoir and carry malaria.**

**Dam and reservoir destroy habitats and disrupt wildlife movement.**

**Trees and vegetation are not removed before the reservoir is created. They rot under water, producing methane, a greenhouse gas.**

**Biting flies breed in the water, carrying diseases such as leprosy.**

**Reservoir floods Indian villages and cuts off traditional hunting and fishing grounds.**

*Brazil plans to build many hydroelectric dams in the Amazon region, supplying cheap electricity.*

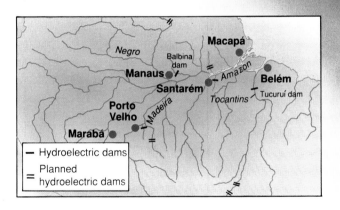

Negro
Balbina dam
**Macapá**
**Manaus**
Amazon
**Santarém**
**Belém**
Tocantins
Tucuruí dam
Madeira
**Porto Velho**
**Marabá**

— Hydroelectric dams
= Planned hydroelectric dams

mostly because the dams have not been planned or built with the local people or environment in mind.

When the Balbina dam was built to supply the city of Manaus, no one took much notice of the possibility that the normally shallow river would rise so high that it would flood the nearby plateau. This has happened, causing hundreds of families to be made homeless. In addition, people living within 10 km of the reservoir now suffer from leprosy carried by biting flies that breed in the water. The traditional hunting and fishing areas of the local Indians have been cut off, and the dam now prevents the migration of turtles that the Indians used to catch for food. It has turned out that the small amount of electricity provided by the dam is very expensive and it would have been cheaper to bring electricity in from outside the region.

*Small-scale mining is common wherever minerals are found in Amazonia. The combined effect of thousands of prospectors can be just as damaging to the environment as a single major mine.*

## GOLD RUSH

For centuries, people have searched for gold in Amazonia, but never before has there been a gold rush like that seen on a small ranch near Carajás in the early 1980s. Thousands of goldminers, or *garimpeiros*, dug into the hill and could be seen caked in mud, struggling up and down slippery slopes carrying soil in old tin cans for washing in a nearby river.

The *garimpeiros* came from all over Brazil and were mainly young workers from the small towns and farms, hoping to strike it rich. As the mud of the Serra Pelada hill continued to reveal huge nuggets of gold, the large mining companies, backed by the government, wanted to dig the hill for themselves. An attempt was made to push the *garimpeiros* off the land, but they stood their ground and, eventually, were allowed to stay.

A lot of gold has also been found in other parts of Amazonia, and on a number of Indian reserves. In 1980, about ten thousand *garimpeiros* invaded the Gorotire Kayapó reserve to work the Cumaru mine. The Kayapó are used to dealing with small farmers and ranchers, and were able to fight for a percentage of money from the mine.

**FIGHTING BACK**

Some Indian tribes are making a determined effort to defend their lands against loggers, gold prospectors, large companies and development projects. For example, the Tukano tribe on Brazil's border with Colombia have lands rich in gold, tin, precious stones and what is thought to be the world's largest known reserve of niobium, which is used in steel making. After many years of contact with colonists, the Tukano have gathered knowledge of Brazilian law. They have used this to halt, if only for a short while, some development projects in the region.

*Gaviao Indians watch a train carrying iron ore pass through their land.*

Other Indians have not done as well as the Kayapó or Tukano in defending their rights to the land. Much concern has been shown over the situation facing the Yanomami people, the most numerous of all the native peoples of Amazonia. Until recently, the Yanomami had little contact with the outside world. They survived almost in isolation by fishing, farming and hunting in the forest, in the tradition of their ancestors. They have strong spiritual beliefs and are led by their healer-mystics, or shamans, who uses many of the rainforest plants for their practices.

The tragedy for the Yanomami is that they live in a mineral-rich region on the Brazilian border with Venezuela. In the 1970s, diamonds and tin were found in Yanomami territory, and in the late 1980s, thousands of *garimpeiros* arrived in search of gold. A vast area of the northern Amazon region, known as 'Calha Norte' or Northern Stretch, has been taken over by the military and government authorities for development. The programme includes new roads, ranches, hydroelectric dams, mining and military bases, transforming the Yanomami territory.

▲
*Fine needles of palm wood are used by the Yanomami Indians as decoration. Inserted into the skin around the mouth, they resemble the whiskers of a jaguar.*

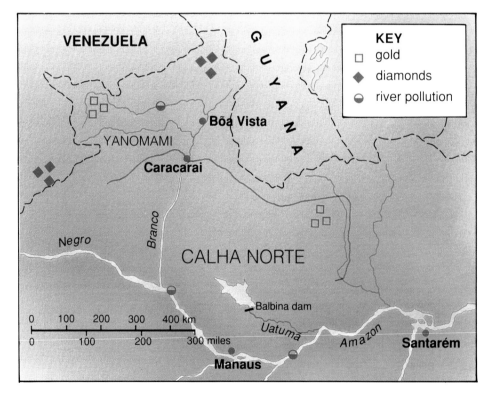

◄
*The invasion of Yanomami lands by prospectors and gold-miners has destroyed and polluted rivers and forest, and introduced new, fatal diseases.*

*Oil and natural gas have been found in western Amazonia, mostly close to the foot of the Andes mountains. Exploiting these resources is difficult and some costly pipelines have been laid. This pipeline lies broken after an earthquake.*

As a result, not only have the Yanomami been deprived of more than three-quarters of their land, but they have also been exposed to diseases against which the people have no immunity. What is more, the mining operations are exposing the Yanomami to mercury poisoning. Mercury is used to separate gold from the earth, and it is being washed into the rivers, poisoning the fish and making the water unsafe to drink. The Yanomami are powerless against the miners, and many people believe that they will not survive this threat to their existence.

Oil and gas deposits have been found in many parts of Amazonia, and in the case of the Waorani people of Ecuador, this has had particularly disastrous effects. Exploration for deposits, mainly backed by foreign business, is taking place both on land given to the Waorani and on a large nearby rainforest reserve set aside for their use. Roads have been hacked deep into the rainforest, attracting thousands of illegal settlers, and further devastation has been caused by spillages of oil and chemicals from pipelines, which pollute many of the rivers used by the Waorani.

The timber industry: many hectares of forest and thousands of trees of no economic value are cleared for the sake of a few valuable hardwood trees. ◄

Ranching and settling: colonists clear vast areas of land for cattle ranches and farms. ►

Road-building: roads are cut into the rainforest, destroying trees and causing soil erosion. ◄

Mining: the discovery of precious minerals in the rainforest has led to huge tracts of land being cleared. ►

Colonists, ranchers, the timber and mineral industries and various development projects have all had a drastic effect on the Amazon rainforest. Figures released in 1992 show that the clearance of the forest had increased by 50 per cent over the previous decade. In the Brazilian Amazon alone an estimated 10 per cent of the forest has already gone. There is general agreement that if the current rate of deforestation continues, there will be no undamaged rainforest outside protected reserves by the middle of the twenty-first century.

It would be too simple to blame the destruction entirely on the people who have tried to make a living out of the resources of the rainforest. The governments of the Amazon countries have all been in favour of development in the region and more often than not have been backed by the industrialized countries of the world.

**PEOPLE WHO CONSUME**

The lifestyle of people in the world's richer countries demands cheap materials to make the goods that are consumed, or used. The Amazon rainforest provides some of these in the form of cash crops, timber, rubber, a wealth of minerals and even meat. Some people believe that each person who consumes these materials, even in the smallest way, is a little responsible for the disappearance of the rainforest.

**INTERNATIONAL MONEY**

In addition, despite meaning well, the governments and finance organizations of the industrialized countries have encouraged the destruction. During the 1960s the idea of international aid was introduced, whereby richer countries could lend money and technical skills to the 'Third World'. In those days, development was seen as the only way to

*Rainforest is cleared for a variety of reasons. When trees are removed, the soil is no longer protected and can be quickly eroded.*

*The USA is disliked by many South Americans and environmental protests were raised against President Bush at the Rio Earth Summit.*

solve the problems of poverty that existed. In the 1970s the international banks were happy to loan millions of dollars to develop agriculture and industry in the Amazon.

**TRAPPED BY DEBT**

Largely through ignorance of the environment and its people, many development projects failed anyway. The Amazon countries have been left with huge international debts to repay. They have little choice but to continue to make use of the resources of their land in order to repay interest on the debts. Some countries have made a stand and threatened not to repay their international debts.

Most governments in the Amazon are well aware that such development is damaging to the environment and that there is a need to help the millions of small farmers and traditional peoples of the rainforest who are trying to survive. Often, however, their hands are

tied by pressure from the military or the powerful landowners who want to continue to develop Amazonia and make money. In addition, sales of other exports (which are not the products of Amazonia) are falling because of the poor state of the world economy.

**THE PEOPLE'S RIGHTS**

An important step forward in the future of Amazonia was taken in Brazil in 1989, when the rubber tappers, Indians and other forest dwellers created the Alliance of Forest Peoples. The aims of the alliance are to defend the people and the forest against developers, and to be involved in the making of future laws that will affect their land. One of the main aims of the alliance is to set up legally-recognized reserves on which they can follow their traditional ways of life. They demand development without destruction. One of the first of these reserves agreed by

# A Global Concern

**Trees trap rainfall. They release it slowly back into the air where it forms clouds again.**

**Trees absorb carbon dioxide from the air. They release oxygen for animal life.**

**At canopy level:** Water falls on rainforest. The canopy protects the lower rainforest from very heavy rainfall.

**At mid-forest level:** Leaves and branches fall to the forest floor.

**At ground level:** The layer of dead wood and leaves is broken down by insects, fungi and bacteria into fertile compost, which nourishes the trees and plants.

**Tree roots and thick forest canopy prevent the soil from being washed away.**

**Rainfall is soaked up by the soil. The trees are able to take up the water from the soil through their shallow roots.**

The rainforest provides a rich habitat for many species. The trees both enrich the soil and prevent it from being washed away. The destruction of the rainforest may also have a direct effect on the global environment. As trees are burnt, a gas called carbon dioxide is released into the air. Like the glass in a greenhouse which keeps the heat in, carbon dioxide traps the sun's heat and stops it escaping back into space.

Large amounts of carbon dioxide recently released by burning fuels as well as trees threatens to make the earth's atmosphere warm up. This could change world weather patterns causing sea-levels to rise with disastrous results.

the Brazilian government has been named after Chico Mendes, the leader of the rubber tappers who was murdered in 1988.

It seems that the welfare of most of the people in the Amazon always comes back to the rainforest. They are as linked into the rainforest system as the millions of species of plant and animal that make up the rainforest itself. Therefore, it is likely that the future well-being of the small farmers, ranchers, *caboclos* and original people of the Amazon depends on a good understanding of the rainforest. Many people believe that governments and planners cannot afford to ignore the knowledge of the forest dwellers.

## THE VARIETY OF LIFE

People around the world agree that it is important to conserve the variety of life found in the Amazon. Scientists believe that if

*Satellite view of 240 sq km Rondônia in the west of Brazil. The areas of cleared forest are the blue regular patterns in the top, centre and right.*

the earth changes in the future, this biodiversity may be the key to producing species of animals and plants that can adapt to new conditions. It is quite likely that clearing one area of rainforest could have far-reaching effects on the remaining area. For example, some species of tree grow hundreds of metres apart. If an area containing one of these trees is cut down, the insects and other animals are not able to transfer the pollen to neighbouring trees and new trees will not be produced, endangering the future of any animals or plants that rely on them.

## A GLOBAL ISSUE

Reasons for concern for the Amazon environment and its people go beyond the boundaries of the region itself. More and more studies of the world's climate seem to show that global warming is well under way. The burning of fossil fuels is thought to be the main cause of global warming (the USA contributes over 20 per cent of the carbon dioxide emissions now enveloping the world), and the burning of the Amazon rainforest contributes a relatively small amount. However, the existence of trees on the scale of the rainforests is especially important. Trees take in carbon dioxide from the air and hold on to carbon in the form of wood, releasing oxygen for animal life in the process. Losing this vegetation-rich ecosystem would mean losing the chance in the future to take carbon dioxide back out of the air. The trees also play an important part in the water cycle. They trap rainfall and release it back into the air slowly, where it forms cloud and rain again. The whole tropical climate depends on this cycle.

Scientists simply do not know what the exact effects of global warming will be. It is more than likely that the world's climate patterns will change. This will not just mean some people enjoying warmer weather – agriculture, industry, in fact complete ways of life may change drastically. Many people think it is simply too risky to let global warming continue uncontrolled.

# · W H A T · C A N · B E · D O N E ?  ·

*I*n 1992, over 150 countries from all around the world took part in an Earth Summit in Rio de Janeiro. Among the issues discussed were development, biodiversity, the importance of the rainforests and the problem of global warming. Although some countries would not commit themselves to plans for the future of the planet, many others have found that they can agree to common aims for the world. Many people hope that the next Earth Summit, in the twenty-first century, will move much further towards global aims on the environment and development.

International organizations that have loaned money for development projects have been criticized for their encouragement of rainforest clearance. Some have now begun to give loans which are intended for environmental research and education as well as conservation projects. In some cases the smaller debts of the Amazon countries have been wiped out in return for their promise to look after the environment. Even so, many poorer nations resent the industrialized countries telling them how to manage their environment and resources.

**Television has played a major part in environmental campaigns in Brazil. A television reporter is interviewing an Amazon Indian who is protesting about businesses and settlers invading his land.**

# The Sustainable Forest

Traditional small-scale slash and burn

Collecting wild rainforest products and small-scale farming of cash crops

Vanilla

Brazil-nuts

Medicinal plants

Palm oil    Breadfruit

Cocoa

Selective logging

Coffee

Rubber-tapping from wild trees

Pineapples

Spices    Bananas

Sugar-cane

Ways of slowing or even reversing rainforest destruction include using more ways of 'farming' the forest without harming it. This is how the Indians and rubber tappers have always cultivated the forest. It is known as sustainable farming because such methods ensure that the forest will continue to provide materials into the future.

Some methods and products are traditional, based on the ways in which Indians have always farmed the forest. Research is also being carried out to develop new methods. Even the timber industry can be managed sustainably. A few selected trees in an area are taken, leaving the rest of the rainforest to speed up recovery.

## SUSTAINABLE FARMING

Using technology and planning to combine tree and crop growing has become known as agroforestry. Some trees that grow in the Amazon region, such as the breadfruit, provide food for both the settlers and their animals. By farming these trees, the rainforest feeds the people that live there, as well as providing a crop that can be sold for export.

Many rainforest plants can supply products which are already widely used, such as bananas and pineapples, a variety of nuts, sugar, coffee and cocoa, as well as spices, peppers, vanilla, chicle – which makes chewing gum – dyes, fibres and oils that are used for perfumes. Small-scale farming may involve more effort and planning, but is likely to cause less damage to the environment. If people who consume the products realize just what they are buying, they may be happy to pay prices that encourage small farmers to change to environment-friendly methods.

*A typical garden plot at the Indian Research Centre at Goiania, Brazil. Students from local tribes spend three years developing farming techniques that are based on traditional methods and new technology.*

*A typical caboclo settlement in the heart of Amazonia. If all the peoples of the rainforest stand together, they can work towards saving one of the richest environments on earth.*

There may be many new products that the rainforest could supply and that can be harvested on a small scale. In the USA, a nut bar and ice-cream called Rainforest Crunch is made from Brazil nuts harvested by rubber tappers in the Acre region. The sale of the bar and ice-cream have helped to pay for a Brazil nut-processing factory. One little-known rainforest plant is the Acai palm. It has a purple-coloured fruit that is used to make a drink and also to flavour ice-cream. The palm also provides edible palm hearts, and its nuts give oil that is used in cooking.

Rainforest plants that may produce medicines are thought to be one of the most valuable resources. Scientists have studied fewer than one per cent of rainforest plants, but already several of them have been used in the treatment of diseases in richer countries of the world.

**PLANS THAT WILL WORK**
The Indians and local peoples of the Amazon have an enormous wealth of knowledge about the rainforest in which they live. Governments, scientists and international organizations are beginning to realize how important this knowledge is in planning the future of the rainforest. Perhaps it is only the full recognition of the importance of people that will bring the Amazon rainforest any future at all.

# GLOSSARY

**Amphibian** Certain animals that live on land and in water.

**Bacteria** Tiny living things that live off plants and animals, as well as dead matter causing it to rot.

**Basin** A large area that is drained by a river and its tributaries.

**Biodiversity** The variety of species that has evolved.

**Bromeliads** A plant family found almost only in North and South America.

**Canopy** The leafy branches at the top of the rainforest.

**Cash crops** Crops that are grown to sell abroad as a main source of money.

**Cultivate** To farm the land, producing crops.

**Deforestation** Clearance of trees over a wide area.

**Development** The growth and change of farming, industry, the environment and people's lifestyles in poorer countries.

**Ecosystems** The web of plant and animal life that lives off and affects its particular surroundings. Ecosystems can cover different-sized areas – from a rock pool to a rainforest.

**Erosion** The wearing away of rocks or soil by the action of water and wind.

**Evolution** The process by which species of animals and plants change over millions of years.

**Fertilizers** Natural and factory-made nutrients that can be spread over the soil making it good for cultivation.

**Geologists** People who study the rocks that make up the earth.

**Habitat** The natural home of particular species of plants and animals.

**Hardwoods** Trees that usually take a long time to grow, making their wood hard. The tropical rainforests are especially known for mahogany.

**Hydroelectric** Producing electricity from the movement of water, usually through a dam.

**Ice ages** Long periods when much of the earth was covered with ice.

**Mangrove** A tree with stilt-like roots that grows in salty shallow-water areas in tropical countries.

**New World** North, Central and South America and the Caribbean.

**Ores** The rough materials that contain minerals.

**Plantations** Large pieces of land, especially in tropical countries, where crops or trees are grown.

**Plateau** A broad, flat stretch of high land.

**Ranching** The rearing of livestock, especially cattle, on large areas of land.

**Reserves** Pieces of land set aside as areas where the environment will be conserved.

**Reservoir** A large lake where water is stored. River valleys are often dammed up to make reservoirs.

**Shifting cultivation** Farming the land for a couple of years, then moving elsewhere to farm, so that the land recovers.

**Slash and burn** The clearing of a small area of rainforest by burning. It is then farmed for a couple of years before being left to recover.

**Smelters** A type of furnace in which metals are separated out of their ores.

**Species** Particular types of animals or plants.

**Sustainable** Able to continue into the future.

**World Bank** The International Bank for Reconstruction and Development, set up to lend money to countries to encourage development.

# BOOKS TO READ

*The Amazon* by Julia Waterlow
(Wayland 1992)
*Amazon Family* by Sarita Kendall
(A & C Black 1987)
*Antonio's Rainforest* by Anna Lewington
(Wayland 1992)
*Brazil* by Evelyn Bender
(Chelsea House US 1990)
*Brazil* by Julia Waterlow
(Wayland 1992)
*Conserving the Jungles* by L Williams
(Evans Brothers 1989)

*Conserving Rainforests* by Martin Banks
(Wayland 1989)
*Indians of the Amazon* by Marion Morrison
(Wayland 1985)
*Let's Go to Peru* by Keith Lye
(Franklin Watts 1987)
*Let's Go to Venezuela* by Keith Lye
(Franklin Watts 1988)
*Rainforest Amerindians* by Anna Lewington
(Wayland 1992)

# ·USEFUL ADDRESSES·

Council for Environmental Education
School of Education
University of Reading
London Road
Reading RG1 5AQ

Friends of the Earth (Australia)
PO Box A474
Sydney
NSW 2001

Friends of the Earth (Canada)
251 Laurier Avenue
W Suite 701
Ottowa
Ontario KIP 5J6

Friends of the Earth (New Zealand)
PO Box 5599
Wellesley Street
Auckland West

Friends of the Earth (UK)
26-28 Underwood Street
London N1 7JQ

International Centre for Conservation Education
Greenfield House
Guiting Power
Cheltenham
Gloucester GL54 5TZ

Oxfam
274 Banbury Road
Oxford OX2 7DZ

Survival International
310 Edgware Road
London W2 1DY

WWF UK (World Wide Fund for Nature)
Panda House
Weyside Park
Godalming
Surrey GU7 1XR

# INDEX